ON FRAME

*Exploring the Depths of Parenting
in the World of Youth Soccer*

Written by Seth Taylor
and Patrick Ianni

An Ianni Training Product

Dedicated to every person
who's braved the wild of
youth soccer. You deserve
to enjoy this experience.

ISBN-13: 978-1724993939

Introduction
A Note from Club President,

Youth sports is a fascinating world. For those of us who work in it, we are faced everyday with some of the most amazing and beautiful experiences as we see kids work hard, bond with each other, and see just what they are capable of achieving. But we also see that there are areas in which we can always improve the culture. We even see areas sometimes where perhaps damage can and is being done to the development of our kids.

In our constant attempt to evolve as a club and provide better ways for our kids to live and learn and our families to thrive, we're really excited to bring the On Frame experience to you. This guidebook is very unique. If you invest some time and eort in the content and the exercises, you will be rewarded with what could be a life changing experience. It will not only have a profound impact on your relationship with your young athlete, but with yourself. On behalf of the club, thank you for being the heart and soul of this club and being willing to always make us better.

Sincerely,

Federico Mariel
City FC President

Foreword
By Clint Dempsey

Some of the fondest memories of my life

are playing soccer as a kid. I still laugh and joke about many of the stories with my friends.

But recently, I've encountered a new experience in the soccer world: being a parent on the sideline.

I have played countless games in lots of different environments, but the feeling of watching your child play is definitely unique. I am the father of 4, and have just begun to see the game from that vantage point. I am definitely not perfect in this role, and often find myself wanting to do exactly what I know I shouldn't.

I think that this guidebook is helpful for all of us parents.

I think we all have one major thing in common: we all want to do what is best for our child and will make crazy sacrifices for them to achieve their goals. However, it is important to take a step back and make sure that our actions aren't preventing the most important element in all of this: our kids having fun and enjoying the game.

This guidebook is something that we can all learn from. It can help us adopt a new framework for helping protect and nurture a healthier identity in our children. To make it in the sports world, I believe that you need to truly love the sport and be passionate about what you are doing.

Let's help our kids learn to love the game so they can have an amazing time on and off the field.

"Through the blur, I wondered if I was alone or if other parents felt the same way I did - that everything involving our children was painful in some way. The emotions, whether they were joy, sorrow, love or pride, were so deep and sharp that in the end they left you raw, exposed and yes, in pain. The human heart was not designed to beat outside the human body and yet, each child represented just that - a parent's heart bared, beating forever outside its chest."

Debra Ginsberg

Introduction

A Different Kind of Parent

In the world of youth soccer, no one plays a larger role in the success of a young athlete than his or her parents. That might not seem like a very profound statement, but when the role is placed inside the context of a performance-based arena like the world of soccer, it takes on a variety of forms that may or may not be understood by many parents. There are nuances and complexities to parenting in this context that are vital to navigate and embrace if we are to raise kids that are not only successful athletes, but happy ones – ready to take on the world however it presents itself when they reach adulthood.

This Guidebook is a tool to educate and equip you for this task. If taken seriously and walked through mindfully, this experience can give you a depth of understanding and a language with which to approach this unique cultural context. It will be a deeper experience than you might expect. But, where our kids are is where our hearts are. That is no shallow thing. The reason the youth soccer world is infected with so much drama and unnecessary conflict at times is because of the extreme depth of love and emotion we feel for our children.

So, for our purposes, we will approach some of these depths within the context of three relationships in the youth soccer world: **Our Kids – Our Coach – Our Team**. First, here is a helpful primer on how to use this Guidebook effectively and the definition of some of the terms you will need to understand in order for you to be a different kind of parent.

How to Use This Guidebook

This Guidebook is a collection of teaching, guided journaling, and action-driven exercises. Each of these things is designed to bring your reflection inward to yourself. This experience is for you and designed completely with the goal in mind of helping you experience as much joy, excitement, and happiness as possible while skillfully guiding your child through this competitive world, so a mindful approach will bring you the most benefit – and bring the greatest benefit to your child. Simply move through the book in order and follow the easy-to-understand instructions over the next few weeks.

Before we begin, let's define some terms that will be helpful for you to understand as you go through the Guidebook. These terms are derived from different therapeutic theories and will give you a helpful language in describing and understanding your experience of being a youth soccer parent.

Awareness
(What is Conscious vs. What is Unconscious)

One of the main goals of this Guidebook is to raise your level of awareness. We use that term to mean simply this: you becoming deeply aware of how the unconscious world is affecting the conscious world at any given moment and in any given person, including and most importantly, within yourself.

Most of what dictates our lives stems from our unconscious world in some way: the world we're not aware of. We tend to orient our relationships because of how we carry our life story deep within us: all the good and all the ugly parts of it. We tend to work from that place, love from that place, and parent from that place... without ever even realizing it. And unfortunately, it is almost always suffering that reveals to us the struggles that we carry in our unconscious world. Those who start to become aware of that fact are more empowered to make choices each day to change and improve their lives and relationships without having to suffer as much. Therefore, the goal of experiences like the one contained in this Guidebook is to help you accomplish a higher level of awareness. Yes, this will mean that deep things will be approached and reflected upon. For it to be effective, it will require honesty and even vulnerability. But again, this experience is for you and you alone.

Trigger

Trigger is an often-used word in therapeutic circles and can have various meanings, but when it is used here, it will be referring to the moments in which *we experience a severe or moderately severe rise in emotion, and the things that cause that rise.* These emotional experiences are many times disproportional to the situation presenting itself. A good example might be something like this:

> **There's a mom on the team that drives you nuts. She talks about the coach as if he and her are best friends and it makes you angry to the point where you find yourself fantasizing about telling her off. You get yourself caught in thought loops and it even feels a bit like anxiety.**

In this example, the word "annoyed" doesn't seem to fit the description of what is being experienced. The truth is that this mom triggers you. Your experience of her and the way she operates is touching on something contained deep in your unconscious. Triggers, then, become the key to unlocking your unconscious world. Each time your child or partner or dog or coach (the list goes on) triggers you, as difficult and painful as that experience can be, you are being given a gift. You are being shown how your story and the things you carry within you intersect with the world around you. These parts of our story are often painful and are accompanied by emotions like deep sadness and intense anger or even intense worry or depression. And this isn't reserved for only those of us who come from difficult backgrounds: it is the human condition.

If we are open to seeing our triggers as a gift, we can start to experience our world with more compassion and less judgement – and that frees us to let people be who they are so that we can be the people we want to be.

The great psychologist Carl Jung said: "We may think that we fully control ourselves. However, a friend can easily reveal something about us that we have absolutely no idea about." Now read that last sentence and replace the word "friend" with the word "referee." This book will help you learn how to see what is being revealed to you by these triggers. And, as you may already know, the world of competitive sports – especially in the context of our relationship with our children – is full of triggers for parents, kids, and coaches.

Speaking of Referees: A Note on the Fairly Obvious

Referees are a necessity in our game and it is fair to say that they tend to be triggers for many parents. A large part of that is obviously because they have such a profound impact on the outcome of a game and thus your child's experience. In this Guidebook, we will not spend much time discussing or reflecting upon the existence or impact of referees, but if we invest in this experience, our awareness will rise to a level that will thankfully allow us to take a deep breath before lashing out verbally at these men and women (and boys and girls) who take the time out of their lives to officiate our kids' games.

Yes, sometimes referees are not as good at their jobs as we would hope. That represents some of the human element of our game. But if our goal here is to produce healthy young adults who live their lives with courage and curiosity, then we can afford to let that poor call go and become aware of our inner experience. Our kids will thank us for it down the road. And they will have had a model set before them of how to handle the many things in life that are out of their control with grace.

Section 1

Your Child

Parents are the ultimate role models for children. Every word, movement and action has an effect. No other person or outside force has a greater influence on a child than the parent.
Bob Keeshan, *Television producer and actor*

There can be no keener revelation of a society's soul than the way in which it treats its children.
Nelson Mandela

Live so that when your children think of fairness, caring, and integrity, they think of you.
H. Jackson Brown, Jr., *Author of the best-selling Life's Little Instruction Book*

It's often said that watching your child play soccer is like watching your heart leap out of your chest and run around with cleats on. For most parents, from the moment our kids took their first step, we've been rooting for them to be awesome at whatever they did and that is no small thing. It is, in fact, very, very deep. Our kids hold the keys to our hearts and all the hidden places inside of us. This is why parenting a young athlete can be so complex: there seems to be almost no way to keep their sporting experience separate from our experience of watching them. When they fail, it often feels like we fail. And when they succeed, it often feels like we succeed. The question is whether that is the healthiest experience for us and our children; and if it isn't, how do we change it?

The answer to that question might hold the key to our kids finding excellence not only on the field, but freedom off of it: to be who they are capable of being, without having to shoulder the burdens we as a society seem eager to heap upon them.

But also, the answer might allow us as parents to enjoy our kids more and worry less.

We've all seen or read about situations where a parent goes too far and does great damage to their children through the sporting experience. Fortunately, most people have enough awareness not to go to extremes, but it is an all too common occurrence that subtle damage is done to the identity development of kids in this arena. And changing that part of our culture starts with each parent being willing to ask some deeper questions of themselves regarding our relationship with our past, our kids, and their performance.

In order to begin helping us approach this issue, we're going to engage in some journaling exercises. If you take your time with this exercise and engage it thoughtfully, you will gain a new level of awareness regarding your relationship with your child and sports.

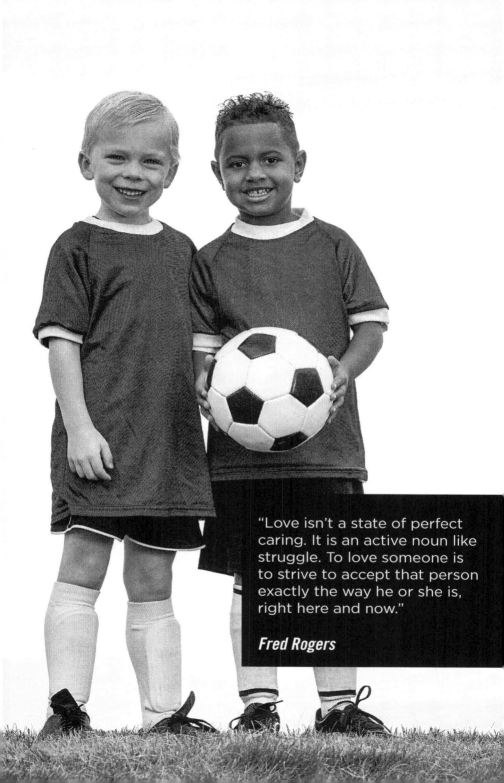

"Love isn't a state of perfect caring. It is an active noun like struggle. To love someone is to strive to accept that person exactly the way he or she is, right here and now."

Fred Rogers

Exercise 1
Remember When

This first exercise will be much like writing and reading an old diary entry. *It is a very simple Top 5 List.*

In our attempt to raise our awareness of our unconscious experience of our children, we must remember who we are and where we came from, as well. Some of these memories may be full of joy and life and some of them may be painful. Whichever they are, breathe deeply and try to remember why they hold such importance for you.

In the boxes, you will write your Top 5 most memorable interactions you had with your parents connected to your sporting or performance universe as a child. Be aware of what your body is experiencing in these memories and, if intense emotions should arise, make a note of that. These observations will be incredibly helpful as you move towards becoming the best soccer parent you are capable of being.

In the space below each box, rate by percentage whether that memory had a positive or negative impact on you. It may be equally positive and negative (50/50)% or one more than the other (70/30)%.

(Helpful note: there is extra note pages at the back of this book if you need more space for writing.)

Memory #1

Positive/Negative [/]

Memory #2

Positive/Negative [/]

Memory #3

Positive/Negative [/]

Memory #4

_____

_____

_____

_____

_____

_____

Positive/Negative [/   ]

Memory #5

_____

_____

_____

_____

_____

_____

Positive/Negative [/   ]

However these memories affected you and are still affecting you, having written them down will be helpful moving into the next exercise where we begin to bring this goal of understanding our children's experience of us and the sporting universe to a new level.

Exercise 2
The Watcher

This second exercise will be an experiential progression from the first. This exercise can be understood as meditative in nature. *Meaning:* it will involve more feeling than thinking, more silence than speaking. The goal is to become what we call "The Watcher."

The next three times your child has a competitive game, training session, or tryout of any sort (or any sport – doesn't have to be soccer), you are going to watch them in a different mode than perhaps you are used to. This time, you will be there to observe your internal experience of the session. The goal is to notice what comes up for you in your thoughts, emotions, and body sensations and over time, to notice patterns that occur in your experience of yourself during these sessions. This can be a very effective tool for raising your self-awareness and even help you see how you may have attached some of your own story to your child's story and their ability to fail or succeed. It might trigger you also – which can be helpful moving into the next two exercises.

Have this book and a pen or pencil with you as you do this and fill in the notes sections provided as you see fit and as things arise.

Here are some guidelines to help you make this an effective experience:

1. Try not to judge your experience as good/bad or healthy/unhealthy. Just allow whatever you experience to be what it is for now. Write down your observations and notice if you feel the need to judge yourself or others.

2. Try to be silent in this experience. If you feel the need to speak or cheer or coach or encourage, simply observe it, write it down, and try to feel (in your body – perhaps chest or stomach?) what is behind that impulse. Don't worry, you'll be back to cheering before you know it.

3. Breathe deeply and slowly. Our experience as we watch our children is first and foremost a *physical* experience. We feel these things in all kinds of physical sensations in our bodies. That is because it is human nature to trap and carry emotions and energies in our bodies in a variety of ways. When we breathe deeply, it helps us slow down and be mindful in the experience.

4. Finally, no detail is too small to notice. This is an exercise to raise your awareness of *you*. So, leave nothing out. Scribble in the margins if you must. There is also extra journaling space in the back pages of this Guidebook, so feel free to write a page number on them and keep going if you need to.

Location _____ Date ___/___/___

Location _____ *Date* ___/___/___

Go back and read your journal entries. Have any patterns developed? What's the good? What do we want to change? How can we change those patterns?

Reflection

As you did the last exercise, what parts of yourself did you see in your child?

Did you see or feel a connection to how you approached performance in your childhood?

Most importantly, could you see or feel how your child is carrying some parts of you on their shoulders?

Remember: these observations are best made without judgement. There is no right or wrong way to do this; there is simply what is. If we can approach it without judgement, we can ask more helpful questions regarding what we want from this experience while raising a young athlete.

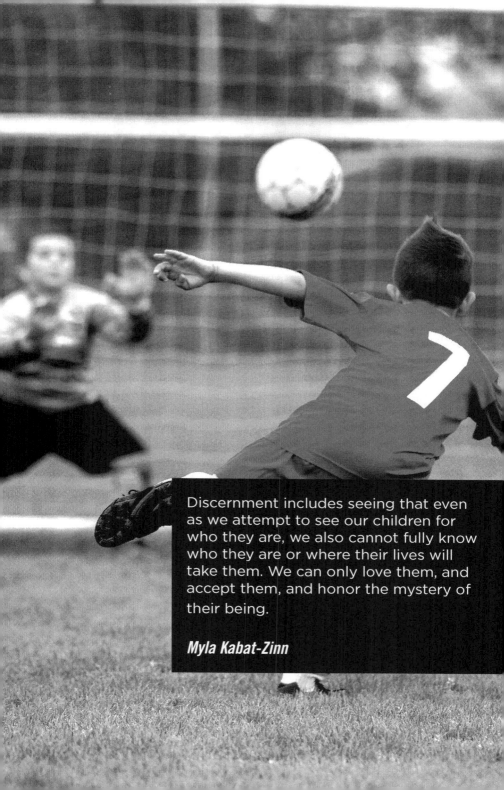

Discernment includes seeing that even as we attempt to see our children for who they are, we also cannot fully know who they are or where their lives will take them. We can only love them, and accept them, and honor the mystery of their being.

Myla Kabat-Zinn

One of the great challenges of parenting is staying connected with our kids as they get older. Part of that is because children naturally need and start to assert more independence as they learn to take the reins of their own lives.

But some of that is also because we forget how to listen to our kids. This might be because parts of us that dwell in our unconscious continue to assert themselves as well, almost without our permission. Like Carl Jung said, "Unless you do the work of making the unconscious conscious, it will dictate your life, and you will call it fate."

The ways that we carry our life story deep within us attaches itself to our kids' life experience and they sense it.

They feel it riding with them in the car after practice.

They feel it standing on the sideline watching them play.

And that naturally begins to erode the trust a child has at a deep level, that their parents can and will love and accept them no matter what.

The reason that last sentence is so important is because the role that the parent plays in the development of a young athlete is not the same as a coach.

The role of a parent is to provide the platform of identity on which a child stands firm so that they can take on whatever task a coach may throw at them without fear.

This identity is made up of one thing: *unconditional love*.

And though all parents would likely claim to love their children unconditionally, the experience our children have in the car ride home after practice often times sounds and looks more like the role of a coach – it is full of critique and expectation. Children begin to hide emotionally from honest conversations with their parents. The standard answer to the question, "How was practice?" becomes "Good" - whether it was or not.

So, in this final exercise of Section 1 of this Guidebook, we're going to spend some time listening to what our kids' hopes are.

Exercise 3
Listening with the Heart

For this final exercise of Section 1, you'll need to make a date with your young athlete. A classic "third place" like a coffee shop would make a great setting for this conversation – the goal being that your child knows by the setting it is taking place in, that this is important.

The directions are simple: Explain to your child what this is – you can even show them the book if you want to. They might get a kick out of the idea that you are working on some of this stuff. Then begin by asking the questions already written in the book. Write down your child's answer so that you will always be able to refer back to it.

Of course, follow up questions will naturally arise and you are free to ask them. The thing that must be remembered and exercised for this to be effective is that you are here to listen and learn, not teach or defend. And that means that you will need to breathe deep and be mindful of what you experience in your body as your child speaks about what they feel and think. This might trigger you. If this is the case, make sure you make note of what you're experiencing in your body and what brought it up in the margins so that you can go back to those things to examine them deeper.

But for now, make this experience as much as possible about your child, allowing everything they think and feel to be fully expressed. Notice their body language and demeanor. These questions may trigger repressed emotion from them, which might manifest as anxiety or even shut them down a little. Do everything you can to communicate safety, but don't force them to open up. Just be with them and wait for them.

But again, above all, *breathe and be mindful* of what you are experiencing. It is in this way that we honor them and we most completely fulfill our role as soccer-parent in equipping them to become the people and athletes they are capable of being.

Our *love* is the foundation and the fuel – and that is all.

What do you love most about playing soccer?
What do you hate the most?

When we talk after a game or practice, do you worry about what I am going to say?

What do you feel when I cheer for you from the sidelines?

When you feel nervous before games or practice, what do you do with that? Would it help if I told you how to handle that?

When I pick you up or you come home from practice or a game, what would you love to be asked? What do I do or say that you wish I wouldn't?

Reflection

on the date with your child

As you went through these experiences, you might have noticed something that you kind of knew was there all along, but perhaps don't regularly examine. Perhaps it was the fragility of your child, which can be surprising sometimes. Perhaps you noticed that they need you more than you thought; maybe you saw that they needed something different from you than what you've been giving them. Maybe you saw more of your own parents in you than you may or may not want to be present. Perhaps the experience has motivated you to go deeper in your own self-examination.

Whatever it was that you took away from Section 1, our hope is that it is something that carries you forward and propels you into a more positive and impactful experience of your child's sporting life.

It may feel like the hard part is over, and perhaps it is, but we're just getting started. Section 2 will be less emotional, but just as important to your and your child's soccer career. Because your coach is now a partner with you in helping your child discover who they are and what they are capable of.

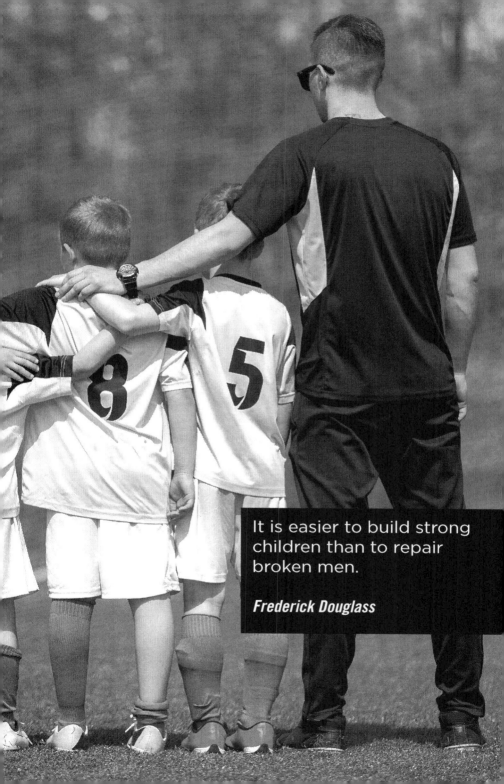

It is easier to build strong children than to repair broken men.

Frederick Douglass

Section 2

Your Coach

That's the beauty of coaching. You get to touch lives, you get to make a difference. You get to do things for people who will never pay you back and they say you never have had a perfect day until you've done something for someone who will never pay you back.
Morgan Wootten

Coaches who can outline plays on a black board are a dime a dozen. The ones who win get inside their player and motivate.
Vince Lombardi

I am just a common man who is true to his beliefs.
John Wooden

As your children grow, you encounter one complex phenomenon after another. Each one of the parenting experiences has the potential to raise your awareness of how you operate deep down and thus make you a more aware and effective parent. One of the more fascinating/terrifying experiences is when you begin to trust your children to perfect strangers, such as soccer coaches, and give them a position of profound authority and influence in your child's life.

We all know this is something that can't be avoided if your children are going to become healthy, independent individuals with the capacity of functioning well in the world. But it's not easy.

In your average soccer club, there are coaches with *tons* of experience, coaches with *no* experience, and everything in between. There are coaches that care about children more than they do about winning and vice versa. And there are those who have been able to strike a balance in their careers.

There are coaches who are parents themselves and there are those who have no idea what it means to love something the way we love our children.

There are coaches that make a lifelong and lasting positive impact on our kids...and there are coaches who do damage. Where your child ends up and who you are required to trust may feel like a crapshoot at times, but thankfully, there are ways to navigate this complex relationship with grace and wisdom so that your child can have an experience where they find a balance between their ground of being (you) and their arena of exploration (their coach).

We're not trying to create perfect lives for our children, with no bumps or bruises, but rather one in which they learn to move as balanced individuals, aware of themselves as people who have a growing set of choices in front of them and the strength and wisdom to navigate those choices as we love them through it all.

And the role that coaches play in this aspect of our child's development cannot be overstated. If our coaches are going to play that role to its full potential, then they must be allowed to be independent, make mistakes, and express themselves. And for them to be able to do these things effectively, we as parents must come to a full understanding of how our unconscious emotions and experiences come into play within this unique triangle of relationship. It is this awareness that will allow us to release some of the control we might otherwise feel the need to exert over our coaches. This awareness can bring trust, wisdom/discernment, and ultimately peace to our experience. And our children will be better for it.

In **Section 2 – Your Coach**, we will engage in exercises that will help us begin to understand this complex relationship, give us tools and language for engaging it effectively, and even a path forward should the relationship bring difficulty. And this will ultimately be felt and understood by your child as a balanced and loving approach to their soccer experience.

I never teach my pupils, I only attempt to provide the conditions in which they can learn.
Albert Einstein

Exercise 1
What would you do?

The following exercise will have an old-school multiple choice feel to it.

We have written five basic and relatively common scenarios that your child may experience. After each scenario, we have written 3 responses that coaches we spoke to have actually encountered in their club coaching careers. Your job is to give the response a "like" (circle the thumbs up) or mark it down as an undesirable response (circle the thumbs down). Then spend a sentence or two explaining why you gave that response.

Finally, each scenario will have a section at the end of it for you to write down what you hope or intend your response to be, should you encounter this situation.

This is about honesty and authenticity in what your experience is. No matter what we understand in our mind is the best thing to do in each scenario, if we don't have the ability to act out of a higher awareness when the moment comes and we are triggered, then we haven't accomplished much through this exercise. The goal then is to be mindful of what you experience **in your body** as you do this. That way your awareness will remain *there* when you encounter things like this in real time.

(Remember – all of these scenarios and responses have happened and are relatively common).

Scenario 1 - Lack of Playing Time

Your child used to be a starter and has now been relegated to a subs-role and even though the coach has stated that he wants to play each child equally because "development is the priority", at times your child doesn't get much playing time in important games.

What should you do?

Explain to your child that the most logical explanation is that the coach must not like him/her.

Have intentional conversations with your child about how they are feeling, how to express their feelings to the coach with true curiosity as to how they can improve, and how to bravely approach their weaknesses as a player so that they can earn more playing time.

Text, email, and call the coach to leave a voicemail explaining that you would like to talk about "how (your child) is doing".

What would you do? Write down your thoughts.

Scenario 2 - Out of Position

You show up to a game and observe that even though your child has always been an attacking player, it seems that the new coach has decided to try them at Outside Back (Defender) without discussing it with you.

What should you do?

Observe that this triggers you, take a deep breath, watch with curiosity, and engage your child afterward with intentional conversation about how they are feeling.

Text the coach from the sideline inquiring as to why he/she made this choice using emojis to hide the fact that you are upset.

Start asking other parents what they think the coach is up to while making a plan to talk to the coach after the game.

What would you do? Write down your thoughts.

Scenario 3 - Where Did the Fun Go?

You observe that your Coach stays calm enough in practice, but when the games start, he/she gets triggered, and tends to yell at the kids and sometimes the ref. You can see that it intimidates your child and it may even be contributing to the diminishing enthusiasm he/she has for the game.

What should you do?

Text the coach from the sideline and
tell him/her to calm down.

Pull your child off the team and incite other parents
to do the same.

Make an appointment to speak with the coaching director seeking guidance on club protocols dealing with these issues while at the same time having intentional conversations with your child about how they are feeling and how they can be aware of their own experience as separate from their coach's experience.

What would you do? Write down your thoughts.

Scenario 4 - Relegation

Your child was dropped to a lower team after tryouts, despite her/his having been on the former team for a number of years. Your child is upset and the whole situation triggers you badly because you just lost a community you had grown fond of, not to mention what this implies about your child's ability.

What should you do?

Take your child somewhere special that invokes a feeling of love and safety and when they are ready, have intentional conversations about how they're feeling. Present them with multiple options for their soccer life and allow them to choose what they want to do, showing love and support no matter what direction they want to go.

File a complaint with all the coaching directors and ask for a meeting to discuss the skewed and biased perspective of the coach.

Pull your child out of the club and begin contacting other clubs in order to get a fresh start.

What would you do? Write down your thoughts.

Scenario 5 - Soccer or Family?

The coach keeps surprising you with extra practices required for your team. You didn't expect this and it's causing problems with your schedule and making quality family time an issue. You're afraid that if you keep your child home, they will fall out of favor with the coach and lose playing time or worse.

What should you do?

Keep your child home for the extra practices and hope for the best.

Email the coach, respectfully expressing your feelings and asking for guidance as to how to strike a balance between his requirements and your family's and child's needs with the intention of doing what is best for your child's mental and emotional health no matter what, accepting whatever the consequence may be.

Start talking to other parents about how unreasonable this is and how something needs to be done.

What would you do? Write down your thoughts.

Exercise 2
Let It Role.

The following exercise is a progression from the last. The goal is to examine what our beliefs are regarding the different roles that coaches and parents play in helping a young athlete succeed. These roles are distinctively different and a great deal of the problems encountered by children in this journey through youth sports stems from these roles encroaching upon one another.

It's worth repeating: the reason this happens is very deep and usually dwells in the unconscious beliefs we have and roles we learned in our own upbringing. And that goes for coaches and parents alike. Many times, coaches unconsciously begin to step into the parents' role just like so many parents spend far too much energy coaching their children. Kids feel this confusion. We can't fix all of that in a few short weeks but if we can raise our awareness of these things, we are more empowered to approach these parts of ourselves with curiosity and courage, knowing that ultimately, our children will benefit.

This exercise features a grid that has various roles in the development of a young athlete written out. Each of these roles are vital for a child to reach their fullest potential.

Under the text, there is a box with sections of writing space:

• *one for parents (left)*

• *one for kids (center)*

• *one for coaches (right)*

Write in each box which percentage of that particular role belongs to the parents, which belongs to the kid, and which to the coach. And then write a sentence or two explaining why you came to that conclusion. For example, a younger child may not be responsible for his/her own nutrition (0%), but a 16-year-old might shoulder more, but not all, of that responsibility (maybe 45%).

Also, be aware that every coach, just like every parent, has strengths and weaknesses, so there is a nuance in this exercise. If, for instance, your coach is a strong communicator with the children, then perhaps your child won't need your support in that area as much, which changes your role and the child's role a little.

That being said, learning to observe your coach's strengths and weaknesses without judgement, as well as your and your child's, is a very helpful component of this experience.

Logistics

Making sure kids have all of the equipment necessary to train and perform well.

Parents [ ] **%**   *Kids* [ ] **%**   *Coach* [ ] **%**

Reasons why: _____

_____

_____

_____

Nutrition

Making sure that kids take care of their bodies in regard to sleep, food, fitness, and hydration.

Parents [ ] **%**   *Kids* [ ] **%**   *Coach* [ ] **%**

Reasons why: _____

_____

_____

_____

Identity Affirmation

Making sure your kids feel accepted, loved, seen, and heard no matter what they do or believe.

Parents [ ] **%**   *Kids* [ ] **%**   *Coach* [ ] **%**

Reasons why: _____

_____

_____

Critique/Coaching

Making sure that kids receive feedback as to the technical and tactical strengths and weaknesses of their game as well as what mentalities to adopt for training and games.

Parents ☐ **%**   **Kids** ☐ **%**   **Coach** ☐ **%**

Reasons why: _____

_____

_____

_____

Opportunity

Making sure your kids have the right amount of game opportunity to test what they are learning in training and reap the rewards of the time they put in.

Parents ☐ **%**   **Kids** ☐ **%**   **Coach** ☐ **%**

Reasons why: _____

_____

_____

_____

Performance Affirmation

Making sure kids feel that the work they put in doesn't go unnoticed and that those that know them are proud of what they accomplish.

Parents ☐ **%**   **Kids** ☐ **%**   **Coach** ☐ **%**

Reasons why: _____

_____

_____

At this point, you can probably see that there is a distinct difference between the role of a parent and the role of a coach in helping a child succeed. The tricky part is knowing where those lines are drawn and having the foresight, wisdom, and self-control to respect those lines.

The more honest and vulnerable we become in talking about these things with our kids and the other parents on our team, the more this understanding will present itself as the dominant mentality.

Success is never final,
failure is never fatal. It is
courage that counts.

John Wooden

Exercise 3
Listening with the Heart - Part 2

The final exercise of this section – **Your Coach** – will be a progression from the last two exercises. For this exercise, you are going to have another date with your young athlete. Just as before, make it formal enough that they understand the importance of this conversation. After you sit down with something awesome to eat or drink, you are going to show them what you wrote down for Exercise 2 – **Let it Role**. Ask for their feedback and opinions regarding each role and the percentages you assigned and why. Ask what they would change, if anything. Here are some guidelines for the conversation:

• Accept everything they think, feel, and offer without judgement or criticism. This exercise is about listening and learning, not agreement or disagreement.

• Write notes about what they say in a different color pen or pencil than what you had before.

• Understand that the younger they are, the slower you'll need to go and the more you'll need to break down the language.

• Be intentional and focus the conversation on how they feel about what you wrote. Their thoughts will come from that place; and more vulnerability in the parent/child relationship is always helpful.

Hopefully this experience gives you a clear sense of direction moving forward so that you can know what your child needs from you and where you can step back and allow your coach to be who they are and do their job with as much respect, independence, and trust as possible.

In any given club, coaches spend 30%-40% of their time dealing with parental issues.

If we can save coaches even 10% of that energy, they will have more to give our kids and more to give to their own lives when they go home at the end of the night. And that is good for everyone involved.

NOTE: There are circumstances where a coach may do emotional damage to a child. It is rare, but it does happen. And in those cases, the club and our directors have protocols in place to deal with these coaches. Don't hesitate to communicate what you are seeing and pull your child from a practice or game if it is clear there is abuse taking place.

As a club, we do everything within our ability to make sure these outlying situations don't invade our culture. For instance, the coaches in our club each have a Guidebook designed for them as well and, in this way, we are creating a better environment for everyone. But outliers do exist. As a club and community, we can all join together in working towards making sure these instances have minimal negative impact on our kids.

The Courage to Trust

You've probably picked up on a theme in this section:

Trust.

In order to give our children the opportunity to succeed and the foundation to approach life's challenges, on and off the field, we must learn to trust that our love for our children is enough.

We must trust their capacity to handle failure and disappointment as well as ambition and victory.

And we must trust that independent and unhindered coaches are vital to that experience, even if those coaches are different than us and make choices that perhaps we wouldn't make.

We have to learn to release our coach and our kids to build relationships that are independent of us as parents. And if we can do these things, we may find that there is a new freedom in the soccer experience for us as well. Perhaps some of the anxiety of parenting may melt away and we'll enjoy our children and this *Beautiful Game* more.

And finally, perhaps this can be a part of preparing us for the big launch of our children into the "real world" that will be here before we know it.

Section 3

Your Team

Grown-ups love figures... When you tell them you've made a new friend, they never ask you any questions about essential matters. They never say to you "What does his voice sound like? What games does he love best? Does he collect butterflies? " Instead they demand "How old is he? How much does he weigh? How much money does his father make? " Only from these figures do they think they have learned anything about him.

from The Little Prince *by Antoine de Saint-Exupéry*

Never hold resentments for the person who tells you what you need to hear; count them among your truest, most caring, and valuable friends.

Mike Norton

It takes courage...to endure the sharp pains of self-discovery rather than choose to take the dull pain of unconsciousness that would last the rest of our lives.

Marianne Williamson

"Team" is one of those words that flexes and moves with time and experience. The first team you were ever on was you and Mom, working together to make you grow in the womb. Your role was relatively small, but vitally important to the team's success of bringing you into the world. The fact that you are here and reading this is because of the effort of that team. As you've grown, you've been a member of many teams with many different functions and goals – some were athletic, most were not.

It truly does take a village to raise a child or should we say, "a team." *And this new group of parents on this youth soccer team is your team now.* You and the other parents of these young athletes are teaming up to propel your children forward into whatever this experience has for them.

Your Coach is a unique part of your team. The team mission: the mental, emotional, and physical health of your kids. You are the pit crew; the coach is the driver. Without both pieces, the car goes nowhere.

Much like Michelangelo's claim that "Every block of stone has a statue inside it and it is the task of the sculptor to discover it," this parental team is doing the work of chipping away at the barriers that keep our kids from discovering their essence and purpose in this world.

Youth soccer is a wonderful arena that presents us and our children with abundant opportunities for personal growth. The end goal of this work is that when adult life presents itself in the not too distant future, our kids will be able to approach it with courage and curiosity rather than some need to strive for perfection. Perfection is never the goal for the parental team – neither is college or professional soccer. This team is not charged with the task of bringing that about. Should a college or professional soccer career present itself, we can delight in that experience, but we delight in it just like any other dream or goal that our kids set for themselves and achieve. These goals must belong to our kids, not us or our Coach. Therefore, the main goal of this team is to find out just how much we can love these kids and what that love is really made of.

The tricky thing about teams is the fact that you are most likely very different from most of your new teammates and very similar to others. And as most parents know, there are few arenas more prone to judgement than in parenting philosophies and techniques. This is why drama and gossip lends itself rather easily to club soccer teams.

If you put 16 sets of parents with all of their various experiences and ideas in the same place and allow them to observe each other closely for a year, you will most likely have a large sum of disagreements. Of course, this is a natural part of forming and bonding as a team.

The goal of the third and final section of this Guidebook experience is to create some deeper reflection on the meaning of team in this context.

The exercises in this section will help you see how you bring your story, consciously and unconsciously, to the team in both helpful and possibly unhelpful ways. The goal is to finish this section with more clarity as to what is your role on this team and a deeper understanding of just how important it is to your child's success on and off the field.

If people knew how hard I worked to get my mastery, it wouldn't seem so wonderful at all.

Michelangelo

Exercise 1
Remember When - Part 2

This exercise will be a return to the first exercise in the Guidebook. But instead of recalling your experiences in relationship to your parents and sports, we're going to think about our teams.

First, your *Top 3 Teams you've ever been on*. These can be in any arena for any reason – not just sports. The key component is reflecting on why this team was/is as great as it was/is. What are the ingredients that have placed it in your Top 3?

In the first box, explain what the team was, where it was, and when. And then in the lower box, say why it made the Top 3.

NOTE: *If your reason for a team being in your Top 3 was because they were "good," make sure you describe what made them good. The goal with the exercise is to understand what elements of a team we are searching to recreate.*

The second part of Exercise 1 is the *"Not" Top 3*. What were the 3 worst teams you have been on and what made/makes them that way.

Finally, when you are done, there is a box for the three "must do" elements and three "must not do" elements of creating a great team according to your experiences. Sum each of those up in a few words.

Top 3 - Team 1

What, When, Where

Why Top 3?

Top 3 - Team 2

What, When, Where

Why Top 3?

Top 3 - Team 3

What, When, Where

Why Top 3?

NOT Top 3 - Team 1

What, When, Where

Why Top 3?

NOT Top 3 - Team 2

What, When, Where

Why Top 3?

NOT Top 3 - Team 3

What, When, Where

Why Top 3?

To create a great team, I...

MUST DO

1. _____

2. _____

3. _____

MUST NOT DO

1. _____

2. _____

3. _____

Exercise 2
Gifts and Weaknesses

We all have strengths and weaknesses that we bring to any team environment. This exercise will involve doing some self-analysis as to what strengths and weaknesses you bring to the parental team and doing a little planning as to how we can do that better.

Picture yourself on the sideline at games, traveling to tournaments, hanging out with other parents, and serving in the various administrative duties that exist on a youth soccer team. You might have experience with this already, which will influence your self-analysis.

In the first 3 boxes, write down your Top 3 Strengths and how you plan on serving those gifts and strengths to the team.

Naturally, the next three boxes after that are for your weaknesses. The real goal when it comes to our weaknesses is to move more and more into a place of appreciation for what our weaknesses have taught us about ourselves, so take some time to write about what you've learned about each weakness and how it can be disruptive to a team environment.

Strength 1

How I will use it for my team:

Strength 2

How I will use it for my team:

Strength 3

How I will use it for my team:

Weakness 1 _____

_____

What I am learning from it: _____

_____

_____

_____

_____

Weakness 2 _____

_____

What I am learning from it: _____

_____

_____

_____

_____

Weakness 3 _____

_____

What I am learning from it: _____

_____

_____

_____

_____

If you struggled to be able to conceptualize what strengths and weaknesses you bring to your team, feel free to come back to this section at a later date. If we begin to observe ourselves more regularly, it will quickly become easy to recognize our strengths and weaknesses in the soccer environment.

Remember, teamwork begins by building trust. And the only way to do that is to overcome our need for invulnerability.
Patrick Lencioni

Exercise 3
One Final Conversation

Now that we've analyzed ourselves when it comes to a team setting and everything we bring to that environment, we're going to take some time to get to know some of our teammates.

This final exercise of the Guidebook is going to be a natural progression from the last two exercises, but this time, we're going to take the opportunity to sit down with some of our new teammates. The truth is, you're going to be spending quite a bit of time with the parents from your child's soccer team, but it is easy to allow the busy schedules to get in the way of ever actually really knowing any of them very well.

The task here is to sit with at least two (or more) other parents on the team that you don't already know well over coffee (or some beverage). The idea is simple: you're each going to take some time to share with the others what you wrote down in the first two exercises in this section.

The hope is that this is a culminating conversation regarding this entire Guidebook experience. If you can risk a little *vulnerability* and talk to each other openly about some of the things you face in this mutual challenge of enhancing your kids' soccer experience, you will find that an amazing thing will begin to build in your team; coaches call it *chemistry* and it is the #1 key to any team's success.

Notes from your conversation. Write down your thoughts.

Vulnerability is the birthplace of innovation, creativity and change.
Brené Brown

Conclusion

I've learned that people will forget what you said, people will forget what you did, but people will never forget how you made them feel.
Maya Angelou

To be yourself in a world that is constantly trying to make you something else is the greatest accomplishment.
Ralph Waldo Emerson

You must be the change you wish to see in the world.
Mahatma Gandhi

We hope that you've gained something in this Guidebook experience that perhaps you didn't have before. Or perhaps you've released something that you've carried for a while that was inhibiting your ability to enjoy your life or your child like you really wanted.

We all know that a parent's role, centered around a healthy identity development, is foundational for all of life. And the importance of the coach's role in a child's life is paramount to them discovering what they are capable of accomplishing. Remember that kids work very hard internally to keep those two worlds separate; too hard, actually. They do this because it feels for them like the world where they find their safety and value is being invaded by the world where they take risks and test themselves every day.

It is our hope that this Guidebook helps parents and coaches become more and more aware of the fact that our kids need us to release the role that is not ours. The results will be immediate and tangible. Our kids will succeed more on the field and be happier off of the field. They will take more ownership of their game and seek safety and comfort in your love. And ultimately, they will be more prepared for life as an adult in this culture.

If this was helpful for you, perhaps give it a year and go through the book again. Talk to your new teammates on the parental team and share your experience and how it has impacted your thinking. Continue to have intentional conversations with your child about what they're experiencing in your relationship in regard to soccer. This intentionality will keep that relationship sacred and will serve to create a foundation of trust for years to come.

Thank you, on behalf of your child and your team, for investing in this process.

We shall not cease from exploration
And the end of all our exploring
Will be to arrive where we started
And know the place for the first time.

T.S. Eliot

Notes

Share your experice of *On Frame* at
IanniTraining.com.

Also available from Ianni Training, The Coaching Revolution.

The Coaching Revolution is an interactive guidebook, taking you on a journey through your own experiences and perspectives regarding how you approach your vocation as a soccer coach, balancing the need to create competitive teams with the call to foster a love of the game in your players and yourself.

The Coaching Revolution is a one-of-a-kind approach to working through the job's toughest challenges. It is a self-examination of what we bring to the game, both consciously and unconsciously, and gives you tools to maintain and enhance your love of the profession while leaving the unhelpful stuff behind.

THE
COACHING
REVOLUTION

AN INTERACTIVE GUIDE TO FINDING JOY
AND EXCELLENCE IN COACHING

FOREWORD BY PATRICK IANNI
US Olympian & a time MLS Champion

Welcome to the Revolution. Let's get started!
Find The Coaching Revolution on Amazon.com!

Made in the USA
Columbia, SC
18 November 2018